The Usborne book of
Origami
AND OTHER
paper projects

Eileen O'Brien and Kate Needham

Edited by Fiona Watt
Additional projects by Richard Dungworth

Designed by Sally Griffin, Rachel Wells and Vicki Groombridge
Illustrated by John Woodcock and Teri Gower
Photography by Howard Allman

Contents

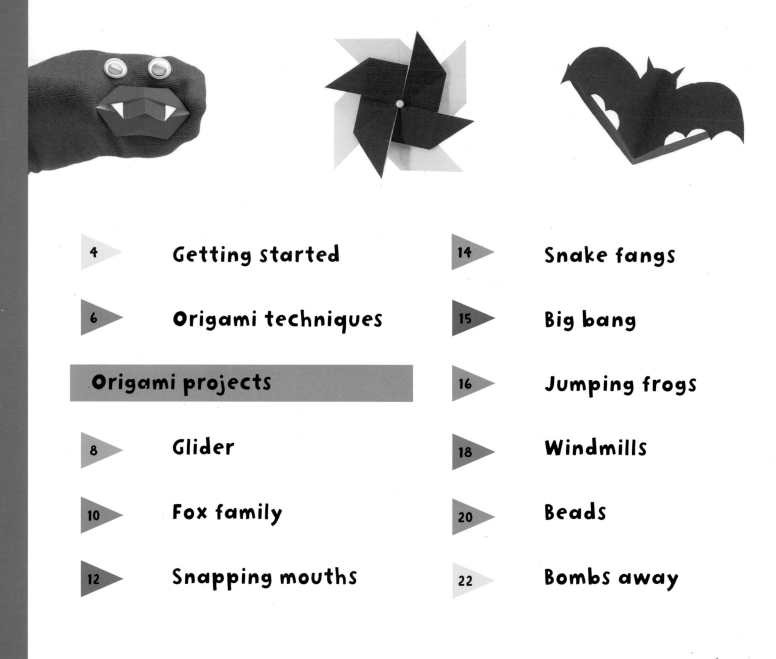

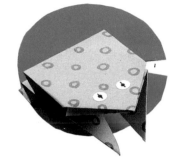

Getting started

This book shows you how to make lots of different origami models. It also introduces you to some exciting pop-up ideas and paper engineering techniques.

What will I need?

You'll find a list at the beginning of each project telling you what you need. Read it carefully to find out the correct equipment and sizes of paper or cardboard.

What kind of paper?

Traditionally, origami models are made from very thin paper, because it is easy to fold and creases well. You can buy special paper for origami from art and craft stores, and Japanese stores. For the pop-ups and paper engineering projects, you'll need to use thicker paper or thin cardboard.

Patterned paper, such as gift wrap, works well.

Some origami paper, like those below, are patterned on one side and plain on the other.

Folding tips

Here are some basic tips to remember when folding paper:

▶ **1** Always work on a hard, flat surface.

▶ **2** Make sure that the corners and edges of the paper meet before you press the fold flat.

▶ **3** Press down on the middle of the fold first, and then smooth firmly out to the sides.

▶ **4** Make sure you fold the paper with the open edges facing away from you.

Hold the edges together firmly as you fold.

Tracing a template

▶ **1** Lay a piece of tracing paper over the template. Hold it in place with paper clips. Trace over the outline with a pencil.

▶ **2** Unclip the tracing paper and turn it over. Scribble thickly over the back of the outline with a soft-leaded pencil.

▶ **3** Turn the tracing over again. Clip it over the paper you want to trace onto. Go over the outline with a ballpoint pen.

Half templates

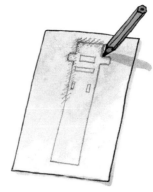

▶ **4** When you're tracing a half template onto a folded piece of paper, line up the red edges on the template with the fold.

Scoring

For paper engineering projects you may need to score lines before you fold them, so that the folded edge will be neat. All the lines you need to score are shown on the templates by the dotted lines.

The best thing to use for scoring is a ballpoint pen that has run out of ink.

If you are scoring a straight line, run the ballpoint pen along the edge of a ruler.

Origami techniques

Origami is a Japanese word which means 'paper folding'. Most of the origami models in this book are quick and easy to make. As the book goes on, the projects get slightly more difficult, so try some of the early ones first.

Decorating

Traditional origami models are created from folded paper only, but in this book you'll find ideas for decorating the folded paper by cutting, gluing or drawing things on the model.

Symbols used in this book

Symbols are used in most of the projects to help you follow each step.

You can see the main ones used throughout the book below:

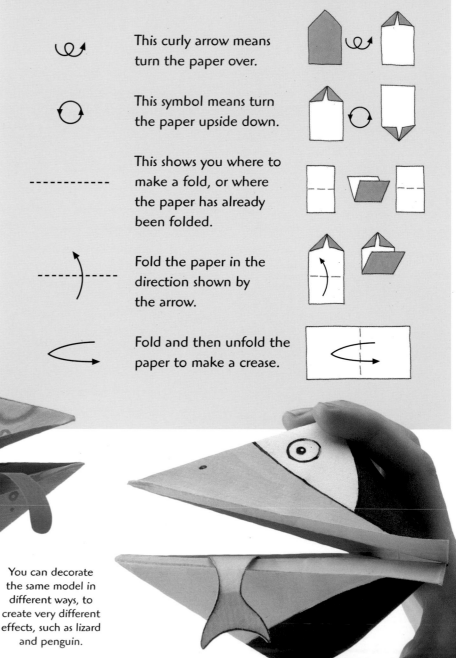

This curly arrow means turn the paper over.

This symbol means turn the paper upside down.

This shows you where to make a fold, or where the paper has already been folded.

Fold the paper in the direction shown by the arrow.

Fold and then unfold the paper to make a crease.

You can decorate the same model in different ways, to create very different effects, such as lizard and penguin.

Use the ideas shown in this book or create some of your own.

These origami lilies are traditional models, but they have straws for stems.

You can see how to make these lilies on pages 24-25.

This lily has been decorated with spots.

Preliminary base

Lots of origami models begin by folding paper in the same way. This preliminary base is used as a starting point for the beads (pages 20-21), the star box (pages 28-29), the lily (pages 24-25), the flapping bird (pages 26-27) and the Christmas tree (pages 30-31). It can only be made from a square piece of paper.

▶ **1** Place the paper right-side up. Fold the bottom right corner up to the top left corner, crease and unfold.

▶ **2** Fold and unfold the bottom left corner to the top right corner. Turn it over. Fold the side edges together. Unfold.

Diagonal creases

Hold here

▶ **3** Fold in half from bottom to top. Hold the bottom edge at both sides just below the diagonal creases.

▶ **4** Bring your fingers together so that the diagonal creases meet in the middle. Four triangles stick out, as shown.

▶ **5** Fold the flap at the front to the right, and the flap at the back to the left. Press the paper flat.

Glider

This glider flies through the air when you throw it in a straight line, and dives dramatically when you throw it high up in the air.

YOU WILL NEED:

a rectangle of paper 30 x 21cm (11 x 8in).
Writing paper, gift wrap, an old magazine or newspaper are all suitable.

You can make a large glider by using a rectangle of paper 42 x 30cm (16 x 12in).

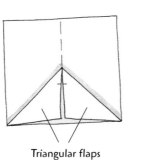

1 ► Lay the paper as shown, with the right side up. Fold the long edges together and unfold them again.

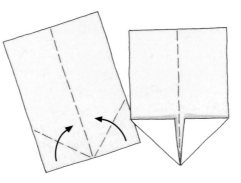

2 ► Fold the bottom corners in to make triangles so that the bottom edges meet the middle crease.

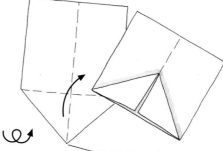

Fold this point up.

3 ► Turn the paper over. Fold up the bottom point as shown above, and crease the fold well.

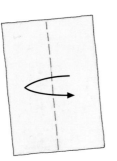

Triangular flaps

4 ► Mark a point about a third of the way down the triangular flaps, as shown in the picture above.

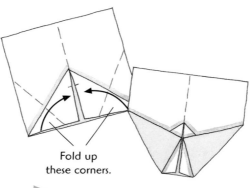

Fold up these corners.

5 ► Fold in the bottom corners of the paper so that they meet at this point. Crease the folds well.

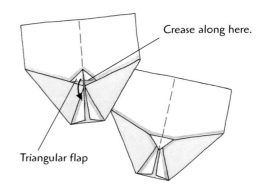

Crease along here.

Triangular flap

6 ► Fold the top point of the triangular flap down as far as it will go, over the triangles made in step 5.

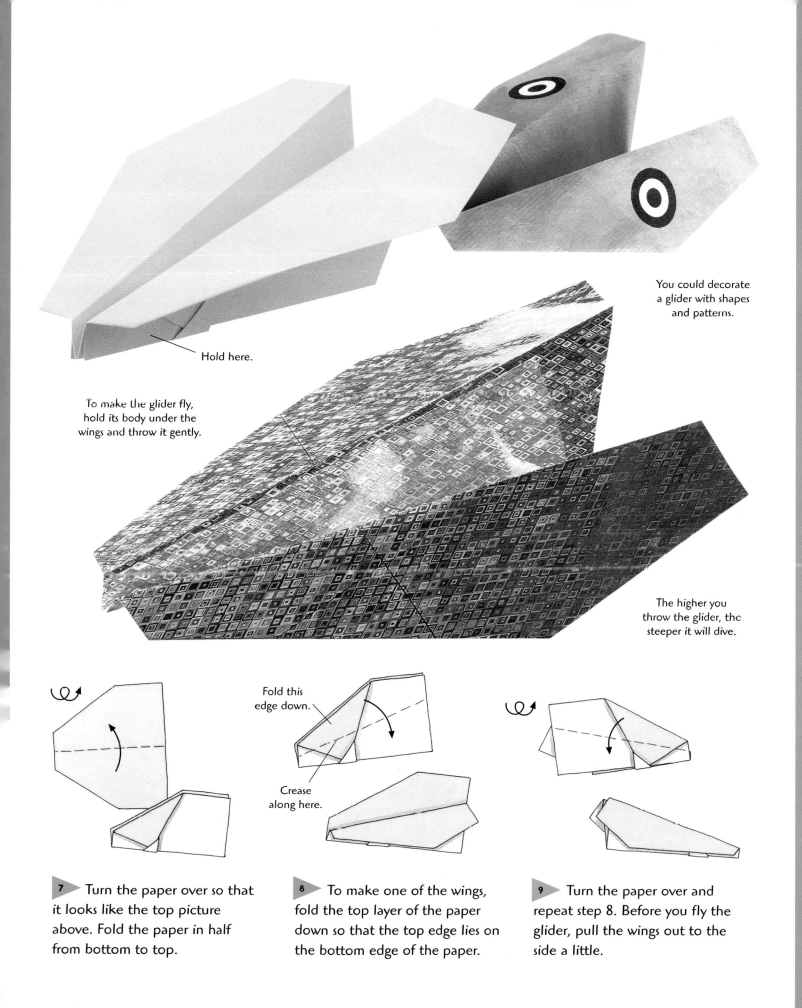

Hold here.

To make the glider fly,
hold its body under the
wings and throw it gently.

You could decorate
a glider with shapes
and patterns.

The higher you
throw the glider, the
steeper it will dive.

Fold this
edge down.

Crease
along here.

7 ▶ Turn the paper over so that it looks like the top picture above. Fold the paper in half from bottom to top.

8 ▶ To make one of the wings, fold the top layer of the paper down so that the top edge lies on the bottom edge of the paper.

9 ▶ Turn the paper over and repeat step 8. Before you fly the glider, pull the wings out to the side a little.

Fox family

These foxes are easy to fold. You can make a whole family of foxes by using the paper sizes shown on the opposite page. You could use gift wrap or decorate your own paper before you fold it.

YOU WILL NEED:

a square piece of paper, 15 x 15cm (6 x 6in) is a good size to start with.

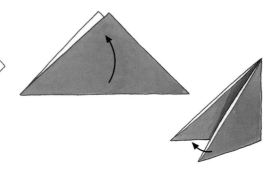

1 ▶ Lay the paper on a flat surface with its wrong side facing up. Turn it so that one corner is at the bottom.

2 ▶ Fold the bottom corner to the top and crease along the middle. Now fold the paper in half from right to left.

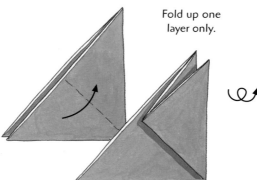

Fold up one layer only.

3 ▶ Bring the top layer of the bottom left corner up to meet the top point. Make sure all the edges meet.

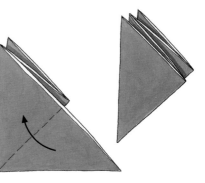

4 ▶ Then, turn the paper over and repeat step 3 very neatly on the other side, as shown in the picture above.

You could use spotted or striped paper.

Use a thick felt-tip pen to draw stripes.

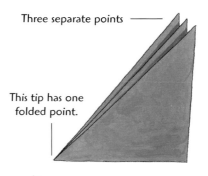

Three separate points

This tip has one folded point.

5 ▶ Lay the triangle as shown above, with the longest edge on the left and the tip with three points, at the top.

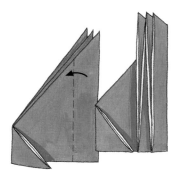

It's a little hard to fold as it's a thick layer.

6 ▶ To make the tail, fold the bottom left corner as shown by the dotted line and arrow in the picture above.

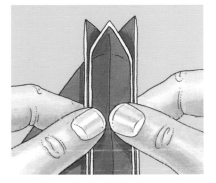

8 ▶ Separate the layers of paper in the flap you folded in the last step so that there are four layers on each side.

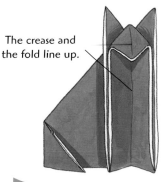

The crease and the fold line up.

10 ▶ To make the fox's head, squash the middle point flat. The crease in the head should line up with the middle fold.

7 ▶ Continue by folding all the layers of the right side over to the left so that they meet the tip of the tail.

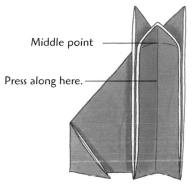

Middle point

Press along here.

9 ▶ Press along the middle fold with your finger so that both of the flaps lie flat. The middle point will not lie flat.

Medium fox

Fox cubs

To make a family

Use different sizes of paper for various members of the family.
Try the sizes given below.
Large fox:
15 x 15cm (6 x 6in).
Medium fox:
12 x 12cm (5 x 5in).
Fox cub:
7.5 x 7.5cm (3 x 3in).

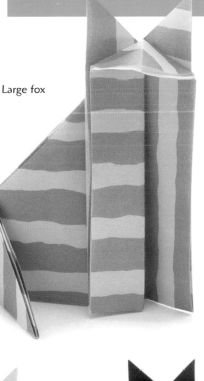

Large fox

Snapping mouths

You can decorate these snapping mouths to make lots of different types of birds and animals. Use the ideas shown below.

YOU WILL NEED:

a square piece of paper 20 x 20cm (8 x 8in). Strong paper such as thick writing paper works best.

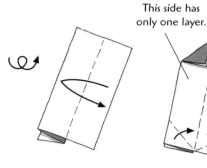

This side has only one layer.

1 ▶ Fold the paper in half from left to right. Then, fold the top layer back so that the right edge meets the middle fold.

2 ▶ Turn the paper over. Fold the top layer back to the folded edge. Crease it, then unfold this layer.

3 ▶ Neatly fold all the corners into the middle crease. Then, fold the right side over on to the left.

To make the mouth snap, hold the back of the head between your fingers and thumb and snap it closed.

Draw or glue on eyes.

Paint your hand and arm with face paints.

For a mouse mouth, leave out steps 4-6 above, and glue on large ears.

Cut through both layers.

Start folding at the slit.

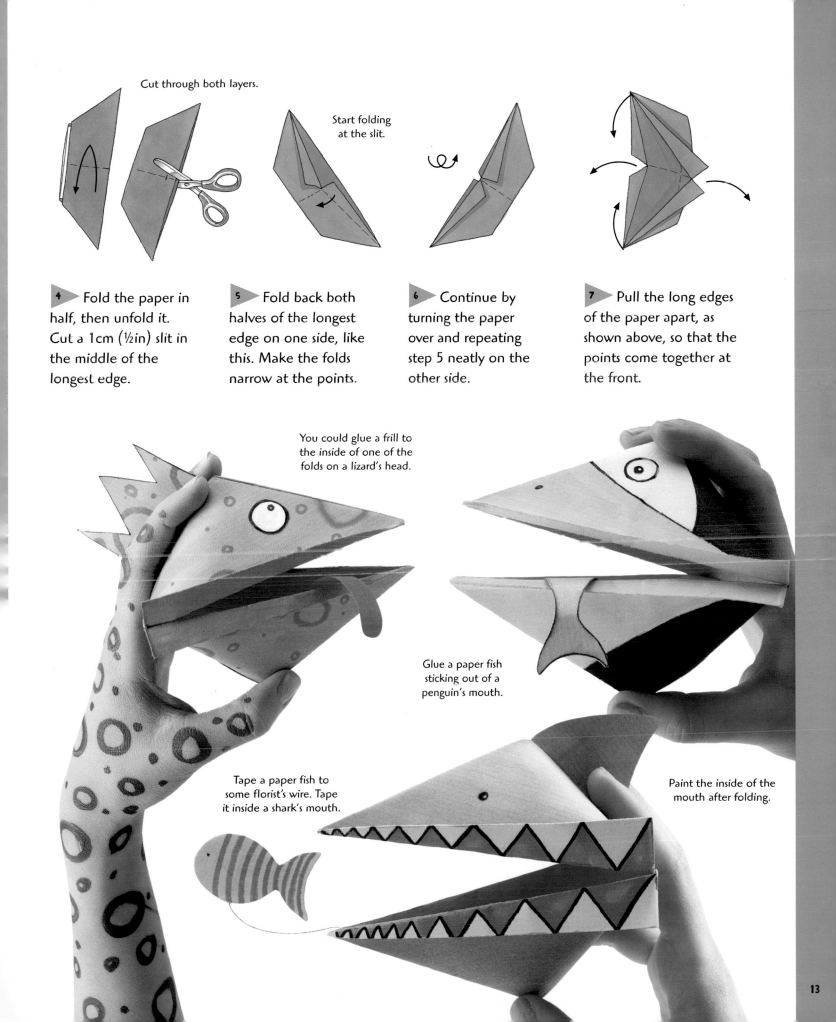

4 ▶ Fold the paper in half, then unfold it. Cut a 1cm (½in) slit in the middle of the longest edge.

5 ▶ Fold back both halves of the longest edge on one side, like this. Make the folds narrow at the points.

6 ▶ Continue by turning the paper over and repeating step 5 neatly on the other side.

7 ▶ Pull the long edges of the paper apart, as shown above, so that the points come together at the front.

You could glue a frill to the inside of one of the folds on a lizard's head.

Glue a paper fish sticking out of a penguin's mouth.

Tape a paper fish to some florist's wire. Tape it inside a shark's mouth.

Paint the inside of the mouth after folding.

Snake fangs

YOU WILL NEED:

a rectangle of paper twice as long as it is wide, for example, 8 x 16cm (3 x 6in). Use paper that is white on one side.

Wear a sock on your hand for a snake's body.

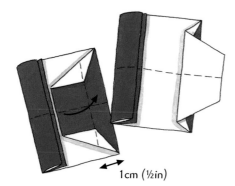

Glue or sew on eyes.

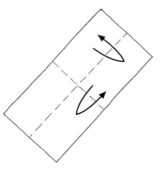

1 ▸ With the white side up, fold the long edges together and crease. Unfold the paper. Fold the short edges together in the same way. Then, unfold them.

2 ▸ Fold both of the short edges into the middle crease. Now fold the left edge only into the middle again and crease the fold.

Fold this corner.

3 ▸ Fold the corners of the right side toward the middle as shown in the picture above. Then, unfold the corners again.

These are the fangs.

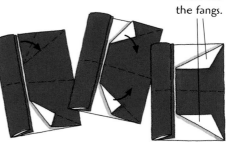

4 ▸ Fold the same corners over to meet the creases made in step 3. Then, fold the triangles over, along the creases made in step 3.

1cm (½in)

5 ▸ Bend the top flap over the right edge, making a crease around 1cm (½in) from the edge, as shown in the picture above.

Fold down along here.

These are the lips.

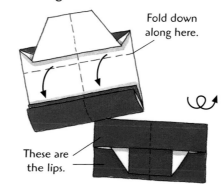

6 ▸ Lay the paper as shown. Then, fold the top of the paper down to the middle so that the lips meet and the white fangs stick out.

To open and close the fangs, hold them at the corners and squeeze gently.

Dent these folds.

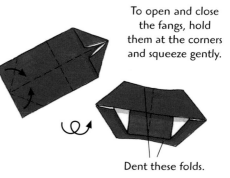

7 ▸ Turn the paper over and fold all the corners into the middle crease. Shape the lips by denting the top and bottom folds.

Big bang

When you hold this banger at one corner and snap it down quickly, it makes a very loud noise. Thin gift wrap or a sheet of newspaper makes a really loud bang.

YOU WILL NEED:

a large rectangle of thin paper, for example, a piece 37 x 50cm (15 x 20in).

Glue on lightning flashes and stars.

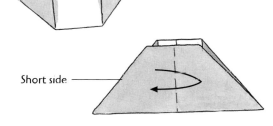

Short side

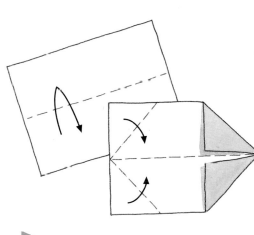

1 ▶ With the wrong side up, fold the longest sides of the paper together and crease, then unfold it. Fold all the corners into the middle crease.

2 ▶ Fold the paper in half along the middle crease. With the long side at the bottom, fold the short sides together and unfold them again.

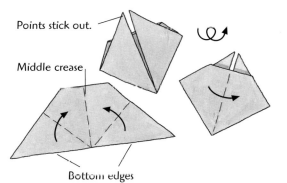

Points stick out.

Middle crease

Bottom edges

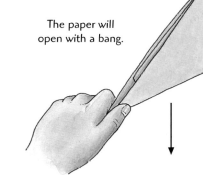

The paper will open with a bang.

3 ▶ Fold up both bottom corners so that the bottom edges meet in the middle crease. Turn the paper over and fold it in half from side to side.

4 ▶ With the long edge facing you, hold the banger at the open end. Then, raise your hand in the air and bring it down sharply.

This striped banger was made from patterned gift wrap.

Jumping frogs

These frogs can jump high into the air. You could cut out a large circle for a pond and smaller circles for lily pads. Try jumping your frogs onto the lily pads.

YOU WILL NEED:

a rectangle of paper 8 x 13cm (3 x 5in); red, blue and yellow felt-tip pens. Use thick writing paper or an old birthday card as it's quite springy.

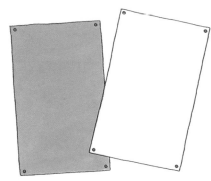

▷ **1** Mark the corners of the paper on both sides with blue dots at the top and red dots at the bottom.

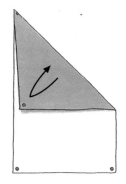

▷ **2** Turn the paper the wrong side up, then fold one blue corner across to the opposite edge. Unfold it again.

Lay the paper flat when you have unfolded it.

▷ **3** Then, fold the other blue corner across to the opposite side in the same way as in step 2 and unfold it.

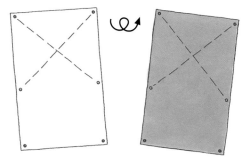

▷ **4** Mark the ends of the new creases (made in steps 2 and 3) yellow on both sides of the paper as shown above.

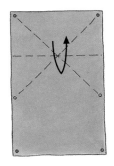

▷ **5** With the right side up, fold the edge with the blue corners down to the yellow marks. Then, unfold the paper.

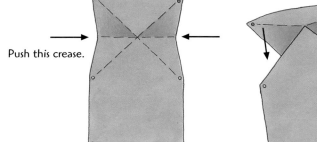

Push this crease.

▷ **6** Put a finger at each end of the last crease and push gently inward. The middle should pop up.

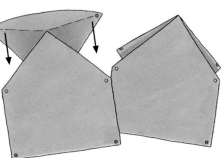

▷ **7** Flatten the blue corners down behind so that they touch the yellow marks. Press this flap flat underneath.

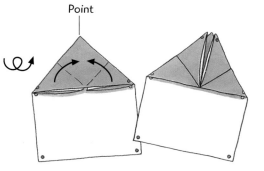

Point

▷ **8** Turn the paper over and fold the two blue corners up to the point. This makes the front feet of the frog.

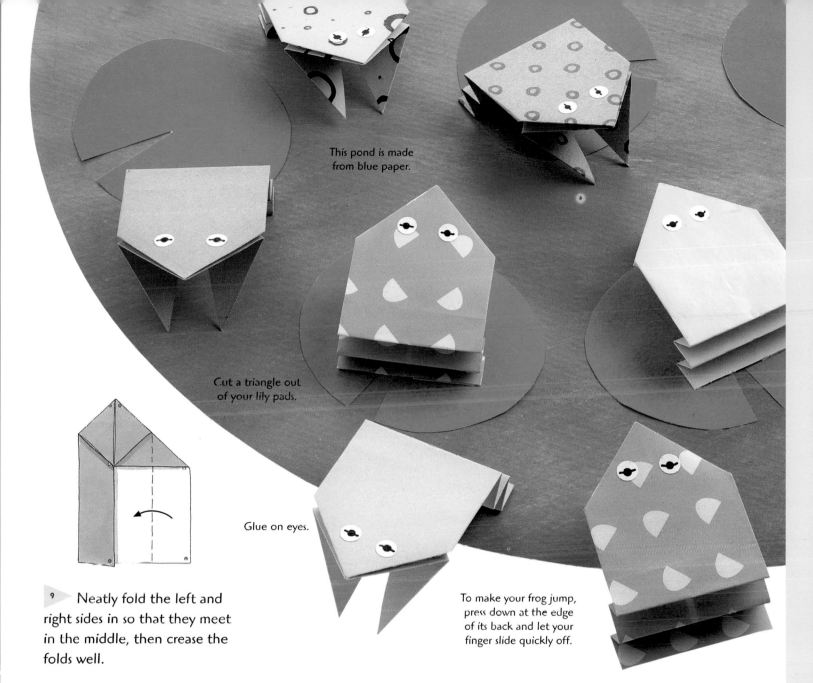

This pond is made from blue paper.

Cut a triangle out of your lily pads.

Glue on eyes.

To make your frog jump, press down at the edge of its back and let your finger slide quickly off.

9 Neatly fold the left and right sides in so that they meet in the middle, then crease the folds well.

To concertina the back legs

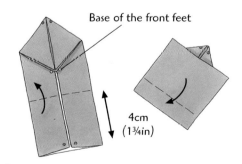

Base of the front feet

4cm (1¾in)

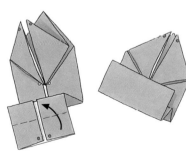

Crease it at this edge.

Pull the front legs out just a little.

1 Fold up about 4cm (1¾in) of the bottom edge. Then, fold this edge back down and crease it at the base of the front feet.

2 Now fold the same edge up again and make a crease at the bottom edge of the paper underneath, as shown above.

3 Finally bring this edge back to meet all the bottom folds. Pull the front legs out so that your frog can stand.

Windmills

These windmills spin when you blow them or walk with them in a breeze. You could decorate your windmill using the ideas below.

YOU WILL NEED:

a square piece of paper 15 x 15cm (6 x 6in); a thin green garden stick, or a kebab stick; a thumbtack or pinboard pin. Light paper, such as thin gift wrap, spins very well.

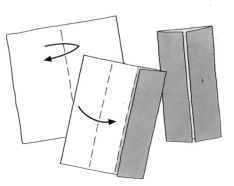

▶1 With the wrong side of the paper facing you, fold two edges together and unfold. Then, fold these edges into the middle crease.

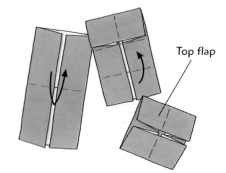

Top flap

▶2 Fold the short edges together and unfold them. Then, fold the short edges into the middle crease. This makes two flaps.

You could make lots of different sizes by changing the size of the squares.

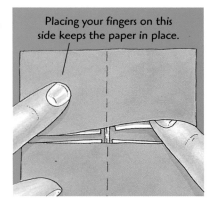

Placing your fingers on this side keeps the paper in place.

▶3 Put a finger between the two layers of the right side of the top flap. Hold the left side of the flap to keep the paper in place.

Try putting lots of windmills in a vase or pot.

To attach a windmill to a stick

Push a thumbtack or pinboard pin through the middle of a windmill. Carefully push the pin through your stick, close to the top. Leave enough room for the windmill to spin around the pin.

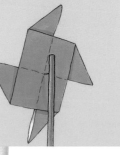

Make a double windmill by putting a smaller windmill in front. Use a square piece of paper 2.5cm (1in) smaller than the first square.

Triangle

These edges meet.

Top flap   Open edges

Pull very gently.

4 ▶ Pull the paper out to the side so that a triangle sticks out. Crease the right edge of the triangle, making sure that the bottom edges meet.

5 ▶ Put a finger between the two layers of the top flap on the left side, and pull out the paper in the same way as the right flap in step 4.

6 ▶ Now turn the paper upside down and repeat steps 3-5 with the other flap. Make sure that the open edges of both flaps meet in the middle.

This is the front of your windmill.

7 ▶ Lay the paper so that the triangles are at the sides. Fold up the right-hand triangle of the top flap so that its point sticks up.

8 ▶ Turn the paper upside down. To complete the windmill, fold up the point of the top triangle on the right-hand side.

To make your windmill spin, blow at the open edges of the triangles.

To attach a windmill to a stick, see the opposite page.

You could paint the stick.

19

Beads

Origami beads are made up of two halves which are joined together.

YOU WILL NEED:

two square pieces of paper, both the same size.
The finished bead will be the same length as one side of the square. If you start with two pieces of paper, 10 x 10cm (4 x 4in), the finished bead will be 10cm (4in) long.

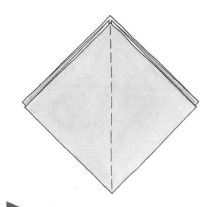

1 ▶ To make half of a bead, first make a preliminary base, as shown on page 7, from one square of paper.

2 ▶ With the open ends of the paper at the top, lift the top flap on the left so that it sticks up in the air.

3 ▶ Then, put your finger or a pencil inside the flap you just lifted to open it out. Remove your finger or the pencil.

The crease lines up with the edges.

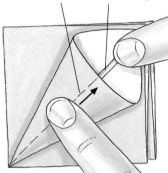

4 ▶ Press down at the bottom of the flap and smooth it carefully, as shown in the picture above.

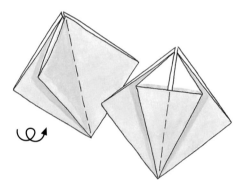

5 ▶ Turn the paper over and repeat steps 2-4 on the other side. Both sides of the paper now look the same.

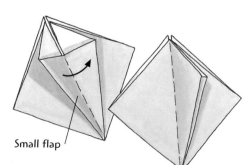

Small flap

6 ▶ Then, fold the small flap on the left onto the one on the right, making sure that the edges meet.

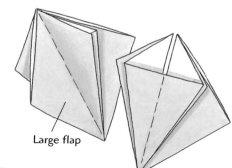

Large flap

7 ▶ Lift the large flap on the left, as in step 2, and repeat steps 3 and 4 very neatly to squash it flat.

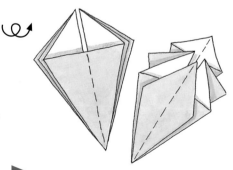

8 ▶ Turn the paper over and repeat steps 6 and 7 on the other side. Fan out all the flaps of the half bead evenly.

A chain of beads

1 Cut a thin piece of wire, such as florist's wire, longer than each bead. Make a loop at one end so that the wire acts like a needle.

2 Thread a long piece of thread through the loop and tie a big knot near the end. Thread a small plastic bead onto the thread.

3 With scissors, snip off the ends of each origami bead to make small holes to thread through.

4 Thread your beads together and tie on a plastic bead after the last one.

Pull the needle through the bead very gently.

To make a necklace or bracelet, leave some extra thread at both ends of a chain.

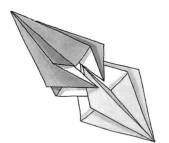

9 Make another half bead. When you have finished, fit the open ends of each half together roughly.

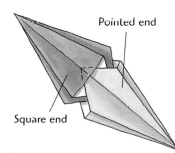

Pointed end

Square end

10 Then, slot the pointed ends of each half into the square ends of the other. Line them up before pushing them together.

You could put plastic beads between origami beads in the chain.

Chains of shiny beads could be used to decorate an origami Christmas tree (pages 30–31).

Bombs away

When you fill this origami water bomb with water and throw it, it will explode and soak whatever target it hits. Make sure you use it outdoors as it's very messy.

YOU WILL NEED:

a square piece of paper 21 x 21cm (8 x 8in) makes a bomb about 6cm (2½in) high. Gift wrap works very well.

You can only throw each water bomb once.

▶ **1** With the paper right side up, make two creases by folding opposite sides together and unfolding them.

▶ **2** Turn the paper over and place it so that one corner is facing down. Fold it in half from side to side and unfold.

▶ **3** Fold the paper in half from top to bottom. Then, hold it in both hands at the spots marked in the picture above.

This can be difficult if you are using shiny paper.

▶ **4** Push the paper in, so that your fingers meet in the middle. There are now four triangles sticking out.

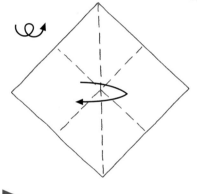

▶ **5** Then, fold the triangle at the front to the right, and the triangle at the back to the left. Press the paper flat.

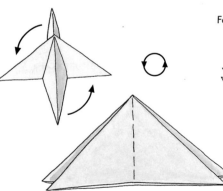

Fold down these corners.

Bottom point

▶ **6** Place the paper with the long edge at the top. Fold the top corners of the top layer down to the bottom point.

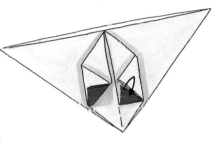

Use chains of water bombs as decorations. See chains of beads on pages 20-21.

To fill the bomb, trickle some tap water into the hole.

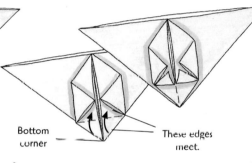

The tips of the triangles meet.

Pockets

7 ▶ Fold the side corners of the triangles made in step 6 into the middle. This makes little pockets shown above.

Bottom corner

These edges meet.

8 ▶ The top layer of the bottom corner has two points. Fold these points up along the dotted lines shown.

9 ▶ Fold the triangles shaded red above along their diagonal sides, up over the triangles with the pockets. Then, unfold them.

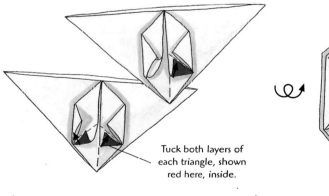

Tuck both layers of each triangle, shown red here, inside.

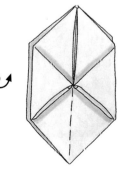

Blow here.

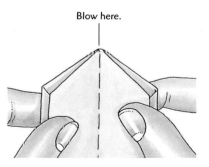

10 ▶ Lift the side triangles with the pockets. Open out the pockets a little. Tuck the triangles below them inside.

11 ▶ Now turn the paper over and repeat steps 6-10 very neatly. The paper now looks the same on both sides.

12 ▶ Pull the two halves of the paper apart. Blow into the hole at the top to puff up the paper into a box shape.

23

Lily

These lilies can be made in different sizes. The first time you make one, use the measurements given below, as the square of paper is fairly large and easier to fold than a smaller one.

YOU WILL NEED:

a square piece of paper 24 x 24cm (10 x 10in).

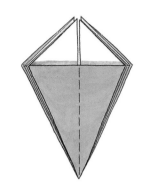

1 ▷ Follow steps 1-8 of the bead on pages 20-21, but do not fan out the flaps. Lay the folded paper flat with the open ends at the top.

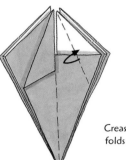

Crease the folds well.

2 ▷ Fold the top layer of paper as shown in the picture above. The top sides should meet in the middle. Now unfold them again.

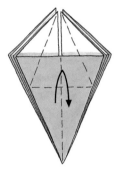

3 ▷ Now fold the bottom point up to the top point. Crease the fold well, as you are folding several layers of paper. Then unfold it again.

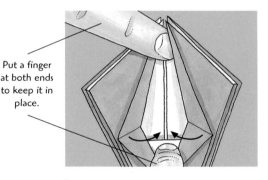

Put a finger at both ends to keep it in place.

4 ▷ Put your fingers as shown and pull the top flap down so that the sides come inward, folding along the creases made in steps 2 and 3.

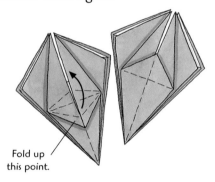

Fold up this point.

5 ▷ Make sure that the edges meet in the middle. Squash the paper flat. Then, fold the point shown above up toward the top of the paper and crease.

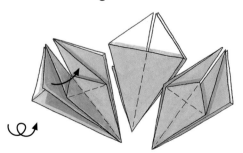

6 ▷ Turn the paper over and repeat steps 2-4 on this side. Fold the top two flaps on the left over to the right and repeat steps 2-4 again.

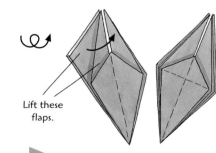

Lift these flaps.

7 ▷ Now turn the paper over and lift the top two flaps on the left over to the right. Then repeat steps 2-4 very neatly on this side.

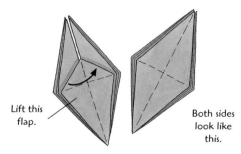

Lift this flap.

Both sides look like this.

8 ▷ Lift the top flap on the left over onto the right. Turn the paper over and do the same on this side. The paper now looks the same on both sides.

Both sides look
like this.

These are the
petals.

Fold along
these lines.

9 ▶ Fold the bottom sides of the top flap into the middle. Then, turn the paper over and repeat this on the other side of the paper.

10 ▶ Fold the top two flaps on the left over to the right. Now fold the bottom sides of the top flap into the middle, along diagonal lines.

11 ▶ Now turn the paper over and repeat step 10. Fan out all the flaps evenly, then curl the petals by rolling each one around a pencil from the top.

If you make a lily from very thin paper, fold it very gently.

For a stem, push the end of the lily into a fat straw that bends near the top.

Make several lilies and stand them in a vase.

Flapping bird

This flapping bird will flap its wings when you hold it at the base of the neck and pull its tail very gently. You could make chains of birds like the ones in the pictures on the opposite page.

YOU WILL NEED:

a square piece of paper, 15 x 15cm (6 x 6in).

1 Make a preliminary base as shown on page 7. When you have finished, turn it so that the open ends are facing you.

2 Fold the sides of the top layer in to the middle so that the edges meet. Then, unfold them again.

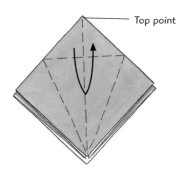

Top point

3 Fold the top point down and crease where the paper meets the top of the two diagonal creases. Unfold.

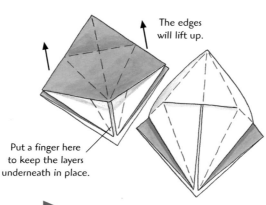

The edges will lift up.

Put a finger here to keep the layers underneath in place.

4 Lift the bottom corner of the top layer of paper over the top point, bending along the crease made in step 3.

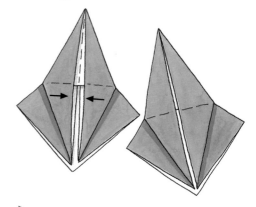

5 Then, fold the two sides into the middle, along the creases made in step 2, creasing from the bottom.

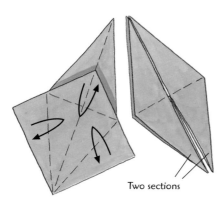

Two sections

6 Turn the paper over and repeat steps 2-5 on this side. The bottom half of the paper has two sections.

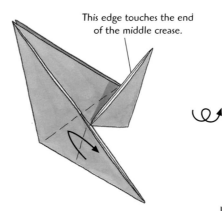

This edge touches the end of the middle crease.

7 Fold the bottom points up so that they stick out at an angle. Crease the folds well and then unfold them.

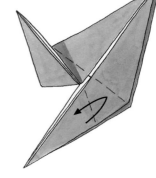

8 Turn the paper over and repeat step 7. Then, fold along the creases made on the other side of the paper.

You could add some small plastic beads.

These chains of birds can be made in the same way as chains of beads on page 21.

To curl the wings, roll them around a pencil.

Put a tiny piece of tape between birds in the chain.

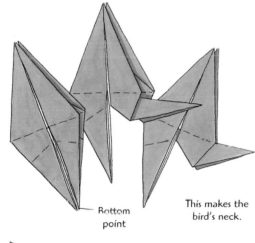

Bottom point

This makes the bird's neck.

If you want to decorate plain paper, do it before you begin folding.

This is the same type of fold as the one in step 9.

9 ▶ Open the right flap. Bend its bottom point up along the creases you have just made. Squash the paper flat.

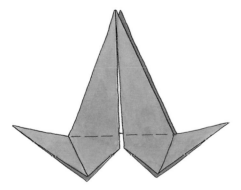

10 ▶ Now repeat step 9 very neatly with the flap on the left. This makes the flapping bird's tail.

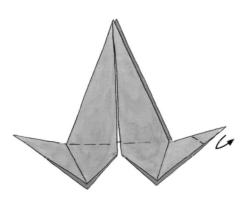

11 ▶ Fold over the tip of the head very neatly in both directions and unfold. Crease the folds well.

12 ▶ To make the head, open out the neck flap and bend its tip down along the crease made in step 11. Squash the flap flat.

Star box

These boxes can be used to store things or you could put presents in them for your family and friends. Try using double-sided paper, or glue two pieces of paper together.

YOU WILL NEED:

a square piece of paper. You could start with a piece 30 x 30cm (12 x 12in).

1 ▻ Make a preliminary base as shown on page 7. When you have finished, turn it so that the open ends are facing you.

These edges meet.

2 ▻ Then, fold both sides of the top layer in so that they meet in the middle, as shown in the picture above.

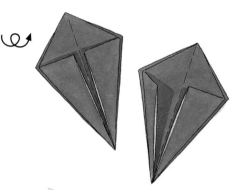

3 ▻ Turn the paper over and repeat step 2 on the other side. Now unfold the left flap so that it sticks up in the air.

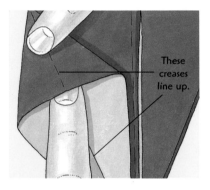

These creases line up.

4 ▻ Open out the left flap, by putting your finger inside. Then squash the flap flat, starting from the top.

You could fill a box with party treats or pot pourri.

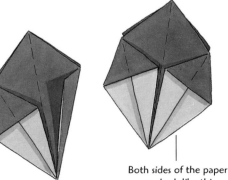

Both sides of the paper now look like this.

5 ▻ Lift the flap on the right and repeat step 4. Turn the paper over, open both flaps again, and squash them flat.

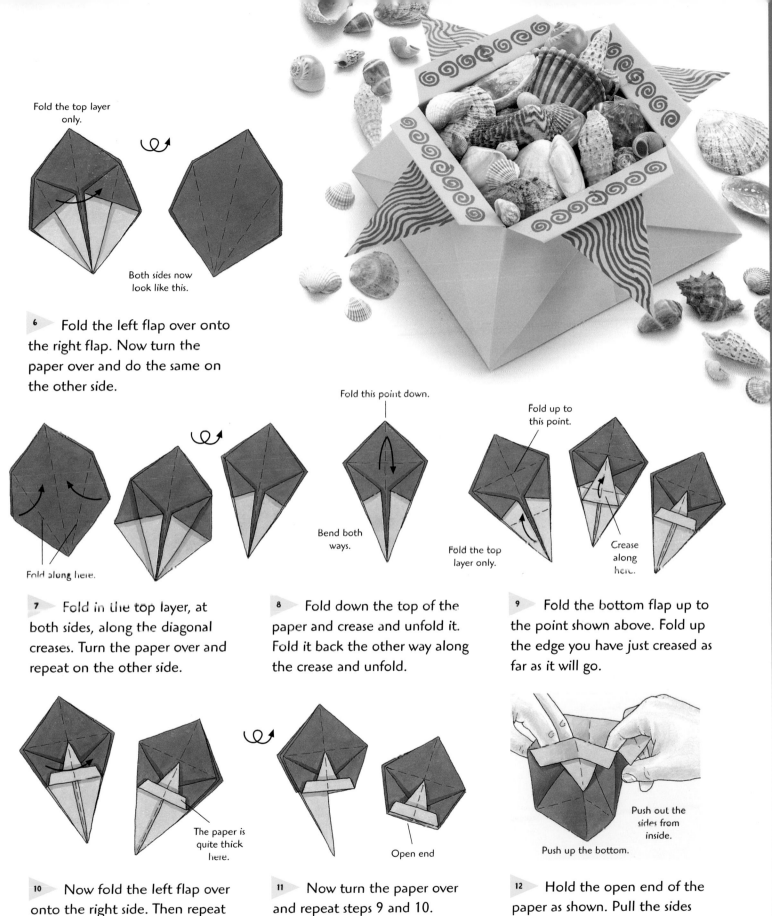

Fold the top layer only.

Both sides now look like this.

6 Fold the left flap over onto the right flap. Now turn the paper over and do the same on the other side.

Fold this point down.

Bend both ways.

Fold along here.

Fold up to this point.

Fold the top layer only.

Crease along here.

7 Fold in the top layer, at both sides, along the diagonal creases. Turn the paper over and repeat on the other side.

8 Fold down the top of the paper and crease and unfold it. Fold it back the other way along the crease and unfold.

9 Fold the bottom flap up to the point shown above. Fold up the edge you have just creased as far as it will go.

The paper is quite thick here.

Open end

Push out the sides from inside.

Push up the bottom.

10 Now fold the left flap over onto the right side. Then repeat the fold from step 9 with the bottom flap.

11 Now turn the paper over and repeat steps 9 and 10. Make sure that all the bottom edges meet.

12 Hold the open end of the paper as shown. Pull the sides apart so that it looks like the finished boxes in the pictures.

Christmas tree

This tree has four sections. For each section, fold the paper into a preliminary base (page 7) before continuing with the steps below.

YOU WILL NEED:

four pieces of paper cut to these sizes:
1. 65 x 65cm (26 x 26in)
2. 50 x 50cm (20 x 20in)
3. 35 x 35cm (14 x 14in)
4. 20 x 20cm (8 x 8in)

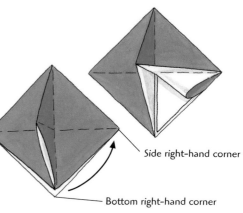

Crease the fold well.

▶ 1 Fold the preliminary base in half from top to bottom and unfold it again. Turn the paper over and repeat this.

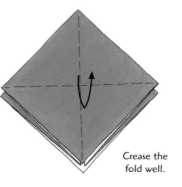

Side right-hand corner

Bottom right-hand corner

▶ 2 Lift the left flap. Bring the bottom right-hand corner of this flap up to meet the side right-hand corner.

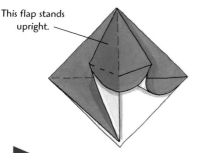

This makes a shelf here.

▶ 3 Hold all the corners on the right together very firmly and flatten the small triangular flap below the shelf.

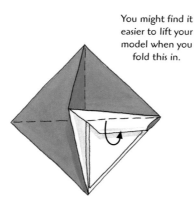

You might find it easier to lift your model when you fold this in.

▶ 4 Bend this triangular flap back under itself, so that it tucks in between the layers of paper above it.

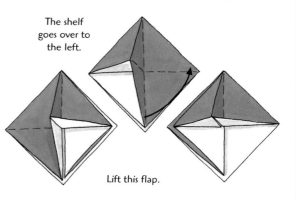

The shelf goes over to the left.

Lift this flap.

▶ 5 Lift the right flap over to the left and bring its bottom corner up to meet the right corner. Repeat steps 3 and 4.

This flap stands upright.

▶ 6 Lay the paper so that the back of it is flat and lift the left flap. The shelves on the right are slightly squashed.

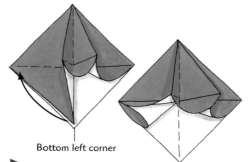

Bottom left corner

▶ 7 Bring the bottom left corner of the standing-up flap up to meet the side left-hand corner of the paper.

▶ 8 Flatten the triangular flap as before, and tuck it into the layers above it. The paper now has three shelves.

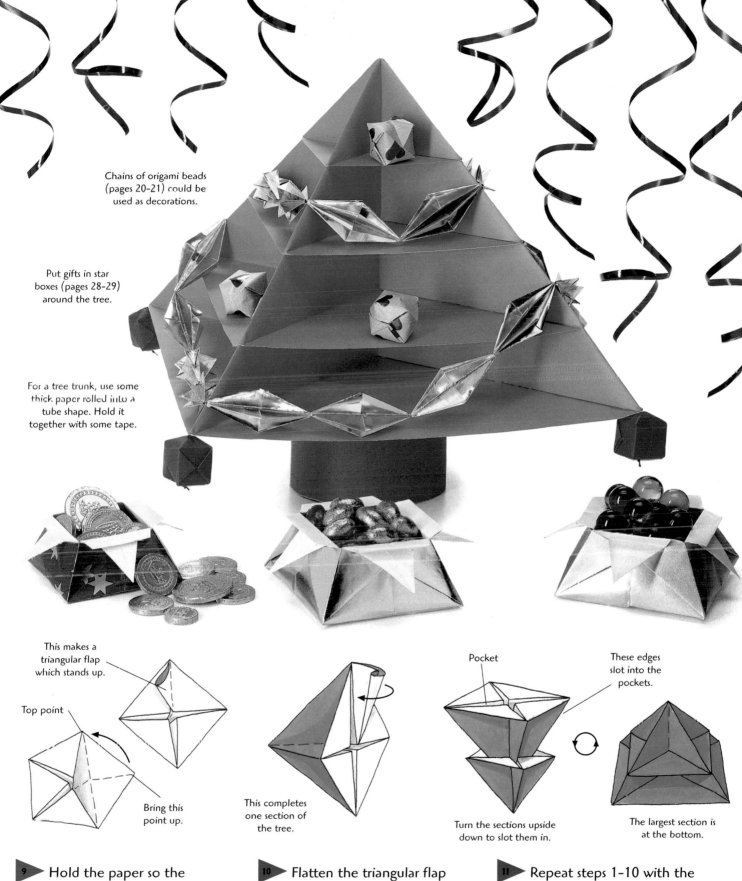

Chains of origami beads (pages 20-21) could be used as decorations.

Put gifts in star boxes (pages 28-29) around the tree.

For a tree trunk, use some thick paper rolled into a tube shape. Hold it together with some tape.

This makes a triangular flap which stands up.

Top point

Bring this point up.

This completes one section of the tree.

Pocket

These edges slot into the pockets.

Turn the sections upside down to slot them in.

The largest section is at the bottom.

9 ▶ Hold the paper so the undersides of the shelves are facing you. Bring the right point up to the top point.

10 ▶ Flatten the triangular flap made in step 9 and neatly tuck it between the layers of paper to the left of the flap.

11 ▶ Repeat steps 1-10 with the other squares. Then, slot the edges of one section into the pockets of the next.

Butterflies and bats

These butterflies and bats spread their wings as you open them. If you have a party, you can use them as place cards.

FOR A BUTTERFLY, YOU WILL NEED:

a piece of thick pale paper 8 x 7cm (3¼ x 2¾in); a pencil; scissors; paints.

FOR A BAT, YOU WILL NEED:

a piece of thick black paper 8 x 6cm (3¼ x 2½); a pencil; scissors.

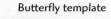

Butterfly template

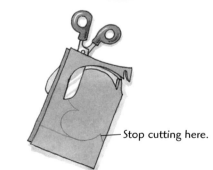

Making a butterfly

Position your tracing like this.

Stop cutting here.

1 Fold the pale paper in half so that its short edges meet. Trace the butterfly template onto it. Make sure you line up the red edge on the template with the fold.

2 With the card still folded, cut along the curved outline of the wings, starting at the antennae. Don't cut along the diagonal fold line.

3 Make a straight cut from the side of the card to the lower edge of the wing. This will cut away the top part of the card around the butterfly.

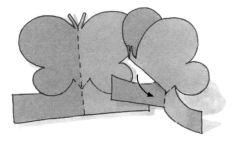

Bat template

4 Fold the butterfly along the diagonal line, first in one direction and then the other, so that the fold is well creased. Open up the card.

5 Hold the card so that the pencil-marked side is facing you. Close it carefully, pushing the cutout part down inside the card, as shown.

Write the name in silver or gold pen on a bat card.

Write your guests' name along the base.

This makes the same pattern on both wings.

6 Close the card completely and smooth it flat to crease all the folds. Add a name. When you open the card, the butterfly will spreads its wings.

7 Dab small blobs of bright paint on the top of one wing. Close the card and press the wings together. Open the card again and leave it to dry.

Making a bat

You can make a bat in the same way. Fold the black paper in half and trace the bat template onto it. Then, follow steps 2-6 for the butterfly.

Pop-up farm

This 3-D cow folds flat inside a card. You can make other farm animals in the same way.

YOU WILL NEED:

thick green paper 18 x 12cm (7 x 4¾in); thick white paper 15 x 9cm (6 x 3½in); pink paper 6.5 x 2cm (2½ x ¾in); a black felt-tip pen; black wool or yarn; glue.

1 ▶ Fold the pieces of green and white paper in half so that their short edges meet. Lay the white paper so that the fold runs along the top.

2 ▶ Using a ruler, draw a line 1cm (½in) from the bottom of the white paper. Fold along the line both ways to crease it. Do the same on the other side.

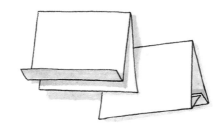

3 ▶ Draw an outline of a cow on the folded paper. Make sure that its back runs along the fold and that both its feet touch the crease, like this.

Don't cut along the fold.

Tabs

4 ▶ Draw a tab at the end of both legs. With the paper still folded, cut out the cow and the tabs. Draw cow markings on both sides.

Make other animals by drawing a different outline at step 3.

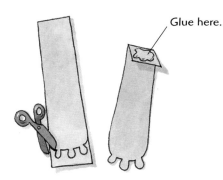

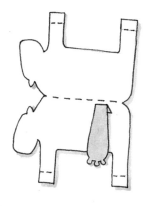
Glue here.

5 ► Cut an udder shape, like the one shown here, at one end of the pink paper. Fold over 1cm (½in) at the other end to make a tab, and put glue on it.

6 ► Unfold the cow. Lay it flat with its decorated side down. Press on the udder tab, so that its fold runs along the inside of the middle fold.

For a hen, make the tail feathers and its comb touch the fold at step 3.

Tape the tail behind the udder.

7 ► For a tail, cut a 5cm (2in) piece of wool or yarn and tape one end inside the crease. Fold the cow. Then, put some glue on both tabs on the side facing up.

8 ► Turn the cow over and press the glued tabs along the fold on the green backing card, like this. Then, glue the cow's other two tabs.

9 ► Carefully close the card and press down until the glue dries. When you open the card, the cow will stand up and its udder will dangle.

For a farmyard scene, make lots of animal cards. Cut grass shapes from green paper and glue them on.

Boxfold cards

One of the easiest ways to make something pop up from a flat card is to use a special fold called a boxfold. This floating spaceman is just one of the many things you could glue to the front of a boxfold.

You will need:
two pieces of thick dark blue paper 22 x 11cm (8½ x 4¼in); thick white paper 6 x 6cm (2½ x 2½in); felt-tip pens; scissors; glue; a silver pen.

You could draw a rocket and glue it on the background.

1 ▶ Fold one of the pieces of blue paper in half so that its short edges meet. Make a pencil mark 4cm (1½in) from each end of the folded edge.

2 ▶ Rule a line 4cm (1½in) long from each mark, at right angles to the folded edge. Cut along both lines. Fold over the flap between the cuts.

3 ▶ Fold the flap the other way to crease it in the opposite direction. Unfold the flap and open the card. Lay it flat, with any pencil marks facing down.

You can copy or trace this spaceman at step 7, if you like.

4 ▶ Pinch along the middle fold on either side of the flap to crease it the other way. Only do this at the ends of the fold, not on the flap part.

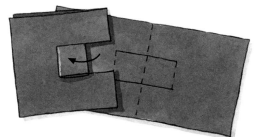

5 ▶ Push the flap down with your finger, like this. Close the card carefully and smooth it flat. When you open it, the flap will pop up to make a box shape.

Don't get glue behind the boxfold.

Make sure the middle folds line up.

Draw or glue on stars.

6 ▶ Fold the other piece of blue paper to make a backing card. Glue the back of the paper with the boxfold and press it inside the backing card.

7 ▶ Draw a spaceman on the piece of white cardboard. Use felt-tip pens to fill in his spacesuit and face. Carefully cut around him.

8 ▶ Glue your spaceman onto the front of the box shape so that he looks as if he's floating in space. Decorate the background with silver stars.

3-D boxfold scenes

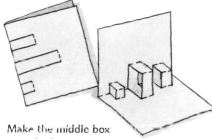

Make the middle box the biggest.

By changing the length of the cuts at step 2, you can make different-sized boxfolds. For a 3-D scene, cut three sizes and glue a picture onto each one.

For a Christmas scene, glue a cut-out fir tree onto the middle box. Decorate the smaller boxes like presents. Add stars in the background.

To make an underwater scene, glue seaweed shapes onto the side boxes and a submarine onto the middle one. Add a seahorse onto a tiny paper spring.

Spaceship lift-off

As you open this card, the spaceship inside swings up as though it is taking off. The backing card is covered with 3-D craters. Templates for the spaceship and its smoke cloud are on pages 46-47.

YOU WILL NEED:

a piece of thick yellow paper 20 x 18cm (8 x 7in); two pieces of thick white paper 15 x 8cm (6 x 3in) and 19 x 5cm (7½ x 2in); coins.

1 ▶ Fold the yellow paper so its short edges meet. Unfold. Mark 5cm (2in) and 7.5cm (3in) down the crease.

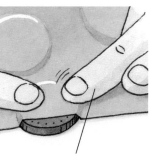

Rub with a fingertip.

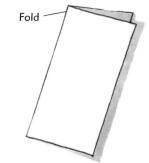

Fold

2 ▷ Using a ruler, draw pencil lines from each mark to both top corners of the paper, to make two V-shapes.

3 ▷ To make craters, turn the paper over and slip a coin under it. Rub over the coin to make each crater.

4 ▷ Fold the big piece of white paper in half, so that its long edges meet. Lay it with the fold on the left.

5 ▷ Trace the spaceship template onto the paper, making sure that you line up the red edge of the template with the fold.

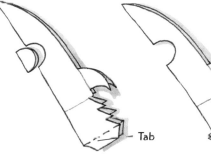

Tab

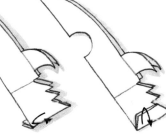

Put the glue here.

6 ▷ Cut around the spaceship, flames and tab. For a porthole, cut a small semi-circle from the fold.

7 ▷ Fold over both the tabs along the dotted line. Fold them to the front and back so that they are well creased.

8 ▷ Unfold the spaceship and decorate both sides. Add a line around the porthole and bright flames.

9 ▷ Partly close the spaceship and fold over both tabs as shown. Put some glue on the bottom of each tab.

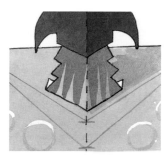

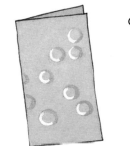

Crease the tabs along the dotted line.

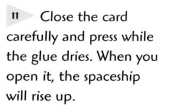

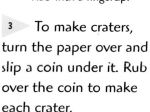

10 ▷ Press the spaceship onto the backing card, so that the tabs fit along the inside of the top pencil V-shape.

11 ▷ Close the card carefully and press while the glue dries. When you open it, the spaceship will rise up.

12 ▷ For the smoke, fold the white paper in half. Trace the smoke cloud template onto it and cut it out.

13 ▷ Glue the smoke cloud inside the card in the same way as the spaceship, but along the bottom V-shape.

Animal mouths

You can use the technique on these pages to make pop-up mouths for all kinds of animals, from wide-mouthed frogs to sharp-toothed dogs.

YOU WILL NEED:

a piece of pale green paper 16 x 14cm (6¼ x 5½in); a piece of thick red paper, the same size as the green paper; white paper.

1 Fold the green paper in half so that its short edges meet. Draw a pencil line 4cm (1½in) long, halfway up the folded edge. Cut along the line.

2 Make pencil marks on the folded edge 2.5cm (1in) above and below the cut. Draw a diagonal line from the end of the cut to each mark.

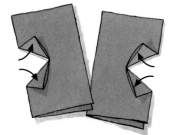

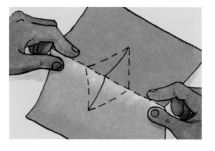

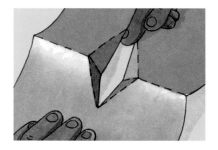

3 Fold along both lines to make two triangular flaps. Unfold the flaps, turn the paper over and fold them in the other direction. Then, unfold the flaps again.

4 Open out the paper and lay it flat with any pencil marks face-down. Pinch the ends of the middle fold to crease them the other way.

5 Hold the paper in place and use one of your fingers to push down both triangular flaps. This will make a diamond-shaped hole, as shown in the picture.

For a beak, cut a shorter, slightly curved line at step 1.

Try making a puffin, peacock, or hatching chick.

Trim off the top part of the card to make it a more interesting shape.

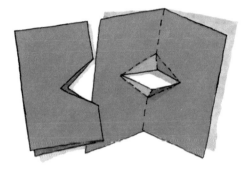

6 ▶ Carefully close the card and smooth over it to flatten the triangular flaps inside. When you open it up, the flaps will close together like a mouth.

7 ▶ Draw a frog around the mouth. Draw a fat body, long legs and webbed feet. Cut out and glue on two circles of white paper for bulging eyes.

8 ▶ Fold the red paper and glue it on as a backing card. Make sure that the folds line up, and that you don't get glue behind the frog's mouth.

For sharp-toothed jaws like these, cut a zig-zag line at step 1.

Pop-up chains

Draw presents or balloons on the backing card of a birthday cake chain.

These pop-up cards are made from simple paper chains. The snowman chain makes an ideal Christmas card.

YOU WILL NEED:

a piece of white paper 18 x 10cm (7 x 4in); a piece of thick blue paper 18 x 13cm (7 x 5in); a strip of white paper 18 x 4cm (7 x 1½in).

1 Fold the white paper in half so that its short edges meet. Fold back each of these edges in turn to meet the first fold. This makes a zigzag fold.

2 Keeping the paper folded, draw an outline of a snowman on it in pencil. Make sure that his arms and toes touch the sides of the paper.

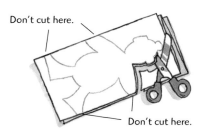

Don't cut here.

Don't cut here.

3 With the paper still folded, cut around your snowman. Don't cut around the ends of his arms and toes, as these will be the links in the paper chain.

4 Unfold the paper carefully. Lay it flat, with any pencil markings on the back. Use felt-tip pens to draw faces, hats and scarves on the snowmen.

5 To make a backing card, fold the blue paper so that its short edges meet. Unfold it and lay it flat. Put glue on the back of the first and last snowmen.

For the monkey card, use yellow paper to make the chain of bananas.

6 ▶ Lay the chain across the backing card, making sure that the middle folds line up. Press the end snowmen down until the glue is dry.

7 ▶ Carefully close the card, pulling the middle fold of the snowman chain toward you. When you open it, the middle two snowmen will stand out.

8 ▶ For snowy grass, fold the thin strip of paper into a zigzag fold. Draw and cut a grassy outline along the top. Glue it inside the card as before.

Different chains

The icing on the cake touches both sides of the folded paper.

Try drawing and cutting out different outlines at steps 2 and 3. Whatever you draw, it must touch both sides of the folded paper so that it will make a chain.

You can then copy or trace these outlines at step 2 to make the monkey or snowman cards.

Snapping crocodile

Hidden inside this model is a mechanism which makes the crocodile's mouth snap as you pull and push its tail. The templates are on pages 46-47.

YOU WILL NEED:

a piece of thick green paper 42 x 30cm (17 x 12in); craft knife; scraps of paper; paint or stickers for decorating.

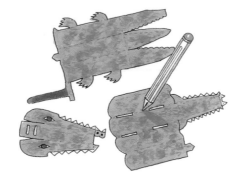

▶ **1** Trace and cut out the templates for the head, body and tail. Trace all the dotted lines and score along them. Decorate each piece.

Glue these tabs.

▶ **2** Fold all the scored lines on the tail part. Glue the two thin tabs on the tail and press the sides onto them. Hold them until the glue dries.

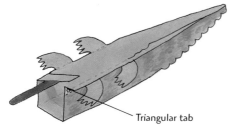

Triangular tab

▶ **3** Turn the tail over and fold the feet at right angles to the body. Glue the small triangular tab on the side and press the end of the tongue onto it.

▶ **4** Fold all the scored lines on the head. Put glue on the two small tabs at the back of the head. Press the part with slots onto the tabs.

Use white paint or correction fluid to decorate the teeth.

For a crocodile like this one, dip a cork in paint and dab it all over the pieces before you make it.

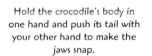

Hold the crocodile's body in one hand and push its tail with your other hand to make the jaws snap.

5 ▶ Fold the scored line at the tip of the nose to make a small triangular tab. Dab glue on it and press on the part with the nostrils.

6 ▶ Glue the top of the tab on the tail section. Slip this tab into the back slot in the head. Turn the crocodile over and press on the tab to secure it.

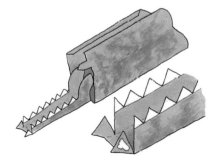

7 ▶ Fold along all the scored lines on the body part. Glue the tiny tabs at the front of the jaw and press the sides onto them.

Glue this tab.

8 ▶ Put the tail and head inside the body and slip the feet through the slots. Glue the tab on the side of the body and press the top onto it.

Glue the top of the tab.

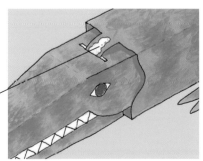

9 ▶ Push the tail forward as far as you can. Glue the tab and push it into the front slot on the head. Put your finger into the mouth and press on the tab.

Templates

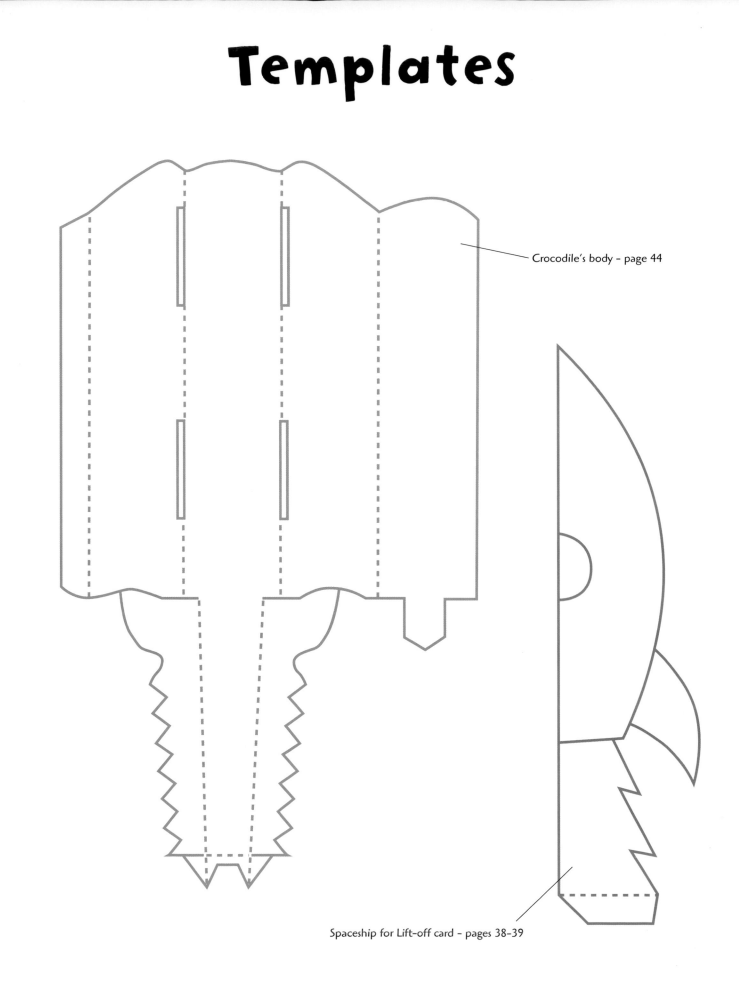

Crocodile's body - page 44

Spaceship for Lift-off card - pages 38–39

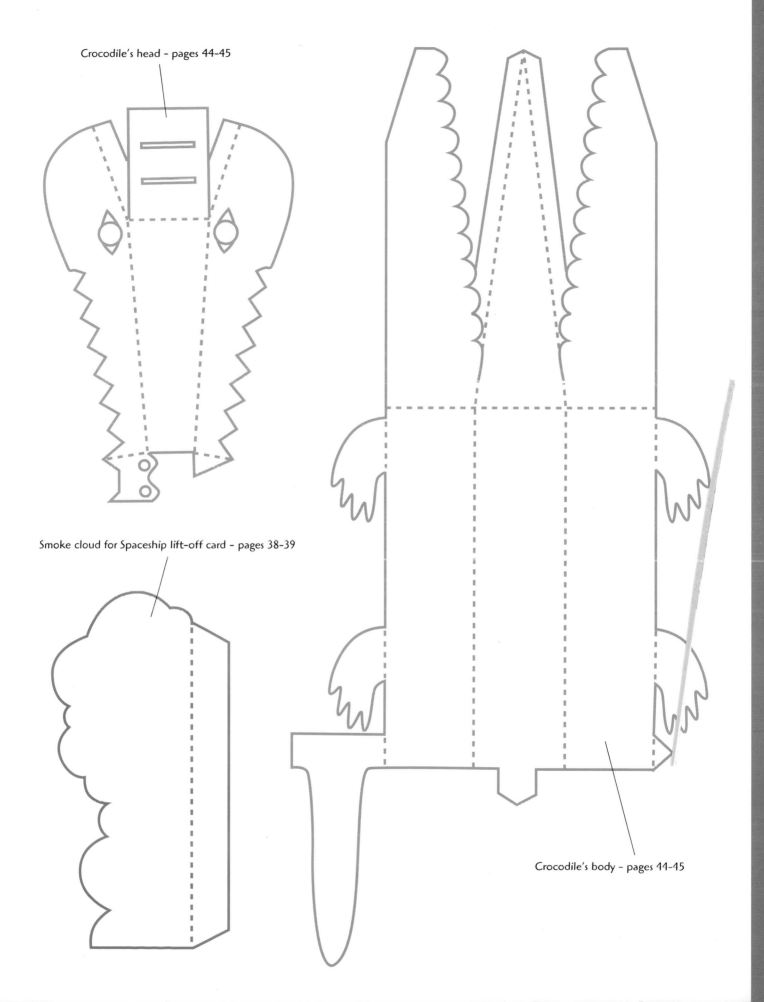

Crocodile's head - pages 44-45

Smoke cloud for Spaceship lift-off card - pages 38-39

Crocodile's body - pages 44-45

Index

Digital manipulation by Mike Wheatley.

This edition published in 2007 by Usborne Publishing Ltd, 83-85 Saffron Hill, London, EC1N 8RT, England. www.usborne.com
Copyright © 2007, 1997, 1996 Usborne Publishing Ltd. The name Usborne and the devices ♀ ⊕ are Trade Marks of Usborne Publishing Ltd. All rights reserved. No part of this publication may be reproduced, stored in a retrieval system, or transmitted in any form or by any means, electronic or otherwise without the prior permission of the publisher. Printed in China.
U.E. First published in America in 2007.